To ————————————————————

Love ————————————————————

# Grandmothers
## *Are Special*

GRAMERCY BOOKS
NEW YORK

This 2005 edition is published by Gramercy Books, an imprint of Random House Value Publishing, a division of Random House, Inc., New York.

Gramercy is a registered trademark and the colophon is a trademark of Random House, Inc.

Random House
New York • Toronto • London • Sydney • Auckland
www.randomhouse.com

Interior design: Karen Ocker Design, New York

Printed and bound in Singapore

**Library of Congress Cataloging-in-Publication Data**

Grandmothers are special : a tribute to those who love, nurture, and inspire.
    p. cm.
    ISBN 0-517-22653-7
    1. Grandmothers—Quotations.  I. Gramercy Books (Firm)

  PN6084.G6G743 2005
  306.874'5—dc22

                                                    2005040398

10 9 8 7 6 5 4 3 2

# Grandmothers
## *Are Special*

It's such a grand thing to be a mother of a mother—
that's why the world calls her grandmother.

ANONYMOUS

Becoming a grandmother is wonderful.
One moment you're just a mother.
The next you are all-wise and prehistoric.

PAM BROWN

Loving grandparents should be every infant's
welcoming committee into a strange new world.

AUDREY SHERINS AND JOAN HOLLERMAN

8

Holding these babies in my arms makes me realize
the miracle my husband and I began.

BETTY FORD

Grandmothers are the people who take delight in
hearing babies breathing into the telephone.

ANONYMOUS

A woman was asked if she had yet made a long trip to California to visit her son and his new wife.

"No," she replied, "I've been waiting until they have their new baby."

"Oh, I see," said the friend, "You do not want to spend money on a trip until then."

"No, it isn't that," the woman explained. "You see, I have a theory that grandmothers are more welcome than mothers-in-law."

EARL WILSON

I'm not a picture-toting grandma—but my grandchildren just happen to be the best-looking children in the continental United States, and you can throw in Canada and the Virgin Islands.

ABIGAIL VAN BUREN

Grandmothers have three major objectives: keep billfold pictures current, buy whatever their grandchildren are selling and give impractical gifts that parents have forbidden them to have.

ERMA BOMBECK

No cowboy was ever faster on the draw than a grandparent pulling a baby picture out of a wallet.

ANONYMOUS

My grandma tells me she keeps the family skeletons in the closet, but I've looked and looked and I still can't find them.

SARAH, AGE 5

Grandma and Grandpa, tell me a story and snuggle me with your love. When I'm in your arms, the world seems small and we're blessed by the heavens above.

LAURA SPIESS

It is as grandmothers that our mothers come into the fullness of their grace. When a man's mother holds his child in her gladden arms he is aware of the roundness of life's cycle; of the mystic harmony of life's ways.

CHRISTOPHER MORLEY

The clock ticks. The fire splutters. The cat sings. There's a knock. Open the door — and there is a smile and outstretched arms and a splodgy kiss and a rush of feet. And a day transformed.

PAM BROWN

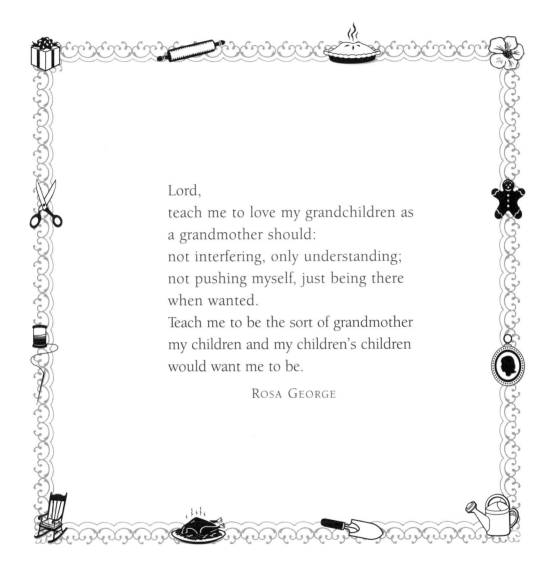

Lord,
teach me to love my grandchildren as
a grandmother should:
not interfering, only understanding;
not pushing myself, just being there
when wanted.
Teach me to be the sort of grandmother
my children and my children's children
would want me to be.

ROSA GEORGE

What is it about grandparents that is so lovely? I'd like to say that grandparents are God's gifts to children. And if they can but see, hear and feel what these people have to give, they can mature at a fast rate.

BILL COSBY

Grandchildren are the best excuse I know to do all the undignified things that are so much fun.

MARION C. GARRETTY

The kind sweet souls who love, cherish, inspire,
and protect their grandchildren are not guardian
angels; they are grandmothers.

BETTYE "MI MI" FLYNN

A house needs a grandma in it.

LOUISA MAY ALCOTT

Parents give grandmas solemn lectures before they
take you out. Some of it gets through — but not
much. They are too busy planning mischief.

JENNY DE VRIES

When grandparents enter the door,
discipline flies out the window.

OGDEN NASH

Why do grandparents and grandchildren get along
so well? They have the same enemy—the mother.

CLAUDETTE COLBERT

Grandmothers and grandchildren have a lot in
common. They are inclined to straggle behind on
walks. They like fancy cakes. They are very fond
of cats and know how to talk to them. They are
given to falling over. They get the giggles.

PAM BROWN

Holding a great-grandchild makes
getting old worthwhile.

EVALYN RIKKERS

A friend of mine was asked how she liked having
her first great-grandchild. "It was wonderful," she
replied, "until I suddenly realized that I was the
mother of a grandfather!"

ROBERT L. RICE, M.D.

Grandchildren are God's way
of compensating us for growing old.

MARY H. WALDRIP

Grandmas are moms with lots of frosting.

ANONYMOUS

So much has been said and sung of beautiful
young girls, why don't somebody wake up to the
beauty of old women?

HARRIET BEECHER STOWE

The great thing about getting older is that you
don't lose all the other ages you've been.

MADELEINE L'ENGLE

The reality is the first child to place a baby
in my arms that grabs my finger, stuffs its foot
in its mouth and smiles at me when I say,
"This is your grandma,". . . gets it all.

ERMA BOMBECK

Few things are more delightful
than grandchildren fighting over your lap.

DOUG LARSON

In the central place of every heart there is a recording
chamber. So long as it receives a message of beauty,
hope, cheer, and courage—so long are you young.
When the wires are all down and our heart is covered
with the snow of pessimism and the ice of cynicism,
then, and only then, are you grown old.

DOUGLAS MACARTHUR

If your baby is "beautiful and perfect, never cries or
fusses, sleeps on schedule, and burps on demand,
an angel all the time". . . you're the grandma.

TERESA BLOOMINGDALE

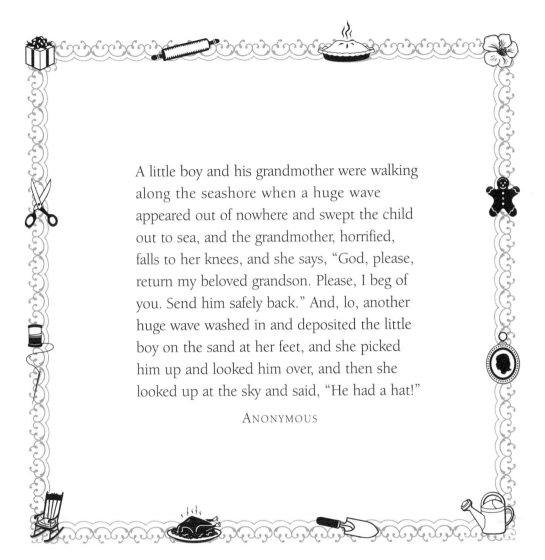

A little boy and his grandmother were walking along the seashore when a huge wave appeared out of nowhere and swept the child out to sea, and the grandmother, horrified, falls to her knees, and she says, "God, please, return my beloved grandson. Please, I beg of you. Send him safely back." And, lo, another huge wave washed in and deposited the little boy on the sand at her feet, and she picked him up and looked him over, and then she looked up at the sky and said, "He had a hat!"

ANONYMOUS

A grandmother is a luxury most of us can afford when we are very young. They say they are our mother's or father's mother — but we only half believe them — for they belong to us.

Their whole existence is dictated by our own. They do have houses and cups and saucers and fruitcake and gardens and cats. But it is as if all they possess is on standby, waiting for us to visit.

They are there to tell us stories, sing us songs, talk about The Long Ago, give us Surprizzles, keep our secrets, show us how to do things, tie up shoelaces—with a bit of pulling. And trail behind with us when our parents are shopping. They are there to be hugged and snuggled, made cups of invisible tea, sung to and wrapped up in blankets. They are there to love us. And to be loved back.

PAM BROWN

Nobody can do for little children what grandparents do.
Grandparents sort of sprinkle stardust over
the lives of little children.

ALEX HALEY

They say genes skip generations. Maybe that's why
grandparents find their grandchildren so likeable.

JOAN MCINTOSH

Everyone needs to have access
both to grandparents and grandchildren
in order to be a full human being.

MARGARET MEAD

A child needs a grandparent, anybody's grandparent,
to grow a little more securely into an unfamiliar world.

CHARLES AND ANN MORSE

Have children while your parents are still young
enough to take care of them.

RITA RUDNER

Perfect love sometimes does not come
till the first grandchild.

WELSH PROVERB

An archeologist is the best husband any woman can have: the older she gets, the more interested he is in her.

AGATHA CHRISTIE

Inside every older woman is a young girl wondering what the hell happened.

CORA HARVEY ARMSTRONG

I refuse to admit that I'm more than fifty-two even if that does make my sons illegitimate.

LADY ASTOR

A grandparent is old on the outside
but young on the inside.

ANONYMOUS

Old people are distinguished by grandchildren;
children take pride in their parents.

PROVERBS 17:6

Even though we were separated by nearly seventy
years, it felt as if she was the earth and I was a
blue spruce rooted and nurtured in her soul.

RITA WILLIAMS

And so our mothers and grandmothers have, more often than not anonymously, handed on the creative spark, the seed of the flower they themselves never hoped to see—or like a sealed letter they could not plainly read.

ALICE WALKER

Her [grandchildren] couldn't defeat her. Or disappoint her. Or prove anything—anything good or bad—about her. And I saw her free of ambition, free of the need to control, free of anxiety. Free, as she liked to put it—to enjoy.

JUDITH VIORST

It's very hard on you, when you are struggling to learn the rules—even of rebellion—to be saddled with a grandma who has outlived those rules. And sits on a wall when her feet ache. And laughs too loudly in the cinema. And talks to strangers at bus shelters. And to waiters.

PAM BROWN

I love my grandma's wrinkles.
Every one tells a story.

TAMMY, AGE 8

An old woman with the soul of a young girl opened her heart to me, because she felt we were kindred spirits. She recreated the world, making it a wonderful place in which everything might happen. In which a tree or a stone was so much more than what we could see with our eyes. She showed me how the veins in leaves were alive and pulsating. And she was the first to tell me that plants cried out when you hurt them.

Liv Ullman

"I'm a flower, Poa, a flower opening and reaching for the sun. You are the sun, Grandma, you are the sun in my life."

KITTY TSUI

We should all have one person who knows how to bless us despite the evidence. Grandmother was that person to me.

PHYLLIS THEROUX

Most grandmas have a touch of the scallywag.

HELEN THOMPSON

When my mother gives me candy
I get sufficient; when my grandmother
gives me candy I get enough.

SAM LEVENSON

Grandma always made you feel she had
been waiting to see just you all day
and now the day was complete.

ANONYMOUS

Grandma was kind of a first-aid station, or a Red Cross nurse, who took up where the battle ended, accepting us and our little sobbing sins, gathering the whole of us into her lap, restoring us to health and confidence by her amazing faith in life, and in a mortal's strength to use it.

LILLIAN SMITH

We would sit together for hours, my grandmother and I. She'd read to me or play board games or dolls. Sometimes we'd cook something fun, like cookies, or we'd go for a walk. She had time for me.

LOIS RABEY

I loved their home. Everything smelled older,
worn but safe; the food aroma had
baked itself into the furniture.

SUSAN STRASBERG

## FROM A GRATEFUL GRANDDAUGHTER

For as long as I can remember you were always there to
teach me how to love others, and how to love myself . . .
and to look for the good in everyone. You were always
there to listen, to hold my hand, and to hug me. Your joy
for life and nurturing care have been a major influence
in my life. Thank you for being my grandmother.

FRIEDA MCREYNOLDS

I really don't think of my grandmother as old,
only well-seasoned.

MAGGIE, AGE 14

So many things we love are you, I can't seem to
explain except by little things, but flowers and
beautiful handmade things—small stitches. So much
of reading and thinking—so many sweet customs and
so much of our . . . well, our religion. It is all you.
I hadn't realized it before. This is so vague but do
you see a little, dear Grandma? I want to thank you.

ANNE MORROW LINDBERGH

Baba: my grandmother. She died in her nineties. She lived alone in Brussels, and sang church songs aloud to herself in the middle of winter. The last summer she came to America for a visit, I took her to a carnival. In the distance we heard the music of the carousel. "I'd like to ride the horse," she said. I held her arm as she stepped up onto the platform. I had to lift her on the wooden horse, which grinned. As the carousel music began, the horse began to bob up and down, which startled my grandmother, then she laughed and laughed as the carousel spun around.

CHRISTOPHER DE VINCK

We danced on and on, unequal partners who in those moments absolutely loved all the inequalities about us, the jokiness, the seriousness. My grandmother was singing: her voice was loud and clear. She spun me for a long time. Our heads thrown back, legs stepping, arms pumping, our fingers intertwined.

MARCIE HERSHMAN

Just about the time a woman thinks her work is done, she becomes a grandmother.

EDWARD H. DRESCHNACK

Psychiatrists have the couch, but Grandma had the porch swing and the kitchen table and a certain way of listening as if you were the only one in God's world worth hearing. Lot of talk these days about the formation of self-esteem and helping children feel valued, but we want the schools to do it. I remember when an hour with Grandma left you feeling like royalty.

PHILIP GULLEY

My grandmother started walking five miles a day when she was sixty. She's ninety-seven now, and we don't know where the hell she is.

ELLEN DEGENERES

I had a hunch we were poor when my grandmother
and I would steal toilet paper from the movie
theaters and take it home with us.

CAROL BURNETT

When we run out of ideas, when we run out of
steam, when we run out of hope—who has ideas
and steam and hope to spare? Grandma!

PAM BROWN

The strength of my conscience came from Grandma,
who meant what she said. Perhaps nothing is more
valuable for a child than living with an adult who is
firm and loving—and Grandma was loving.

MARGARET MEAD

Soon I will be an old, white-haired lady, into whose lap someone places a baby, saying, "Smile, Grandma!"—I, who myself so recently was photographed on my grandmother's lap.

LIV ULLMAN

That's a big problem with some older folks—they have such low expectations of themselves.

SADIE DELANY

A passionate interest in what you do is the secret of long life, whether it is helping old people or children or making cheese or growing earthworms.

JULIA CHILD

It doesn't make me feel old to carry pictures of my grandchildren, but it does make me feel old when I can't see their pictures without my glasses.

LOIS WYSE

A grandmother's stories build strength and provide a foothold for integrity, dignity, and a sense of fearlessness. They give direction, guidance, and self-respect, define limitations, and outline freedom.

FROM *WALKING IN MOCCASINS*

The closest friends I have made all throughout life have been people who also grew up close to a loved and living grandmother or grandfather.

MARGARET MEAD

My grandmother told me to be nice to everyone and always think about how you would feel if you were in their shoes. It's really good advice.

ANONYMOUS

Being pretty on the inside means you don't hit your brother and you eat all your peas — that's what my grandma taught me.

LORD CHESTERFIELD

Grandmas mustn't take sides —but there's nothing to stop them winking.

CLARA ORTEGA

If nothing is going well,
call your grandmother.

ITALIAN PROVERB

If you want to civilize a man,
begin with his grandmother.

VICTOR HUGO

Dearer than our children are the
children of our children.

EGYPTIAN PROVERB

## A GRANDMOTHER'S BEATITUDES

Blessed is the grandmother who makes peace with spilled
milk and mud, for such is the realm of childhood.

Blessed is the grandmother who refuses to compare her
grandchildren with others, for precious is the rhythm of
growth of every child.

Blessed is the grandmother who has learned to laugh, for it
is the music of the child's world.

Blessed is the grandmother who can say "no" without anger,
for comforting to the child is the security of a firm decision.

Blessed is the grandmother who is teachable, for knowledge
brings understanding and understanding brings love.

Blessed is the grandmother who loves her grandchildren in
the midst of a hostile world, for love is the greatest of all gifts.

UNKNOWN

The secret of staying young is to live honestly,
eat slowly, and lie about your age.

LUCILLE BALL

The hardest years in life are those
between 10 and 70.

HELEN HAYES

Old age is no place for sissies.

BETTE DAVIS

A few days before my grandmother died, I was able to speak with her on the telephone. She was dying in a hospital in Brussels, Belgium. "Oh, Christopher," she said. "Oh, Christopher." She wasn't weeping. She wasn't in pain. As she simply repeated my name, all the memories of my grandmother flew out through the international telephone cable: her singing French songs about my grandfather riding a horse, her laughter when my sister Anne and I performed a circus in the attic with our cat, Tiger Lily. My grandmother: her perfume, her worn slippers, her housedress and brown stockings. She liked butterscotch and port and ice cream and card games, and she loved me.

CHRISTOPHER DE VINCK

I believe in loyalty.
When a woman reaches an age she likes,
she should stick with it.

EVA GABOR

When a child is born, so are grandmothers.

JUDITH LEVY

Without doing anything spectacular, you are given your place in the great river of love that rushes underground through the generations and nourishes them.

And newborn grandchildren seem to know this in some mysterious way. They love you for nothing. They run and jump into your arms; then can be comforted and fall asleep clutching your finger or nestled against you. The aesthetic perfections of their tiny bodies is an endless consolation. Your own grey hair or crinkly arms disappear when you gaze on their shining locks and smooth skin. They give you reality. They show you the meaning of life by tumbling you into that river of love.

BETSY BLAIR

If becoming a grandmother was only a matter of choice, I should advise every one of you straight away to become one. There is no fun for old people like it!

HANNAH WHITHALL SMITH

The joy of interacting with grandchildren is a bonus none of us deserves, but how fortunate we are that God sent these gifts along.

BILL AND PAT COLEMAN

To show a child what had once delighted you, to find the child's delight added to your own, so that there is now a double delight seen in the glow of trust and affection, this is happiness.

J. B. PRIESTLY

It wasn't so tough being a good grandma.

Just a week ago she hadn't known the secret.

 But now she did.

Being a grandma just means having a good time.

The really amazing part was that winning the heart of a grandson wasn't really so different from winning the heart of any man.

What male ever failed to respond to a woman who was good to him?

What man ever said no to a woman who always said yes?

LOIS WYSE

A grandmother is a babysitter who
watches the kids instead of the television.

ANONYMOUS

Not all of us think grandkids are the greatest—but
that was before I met mine.

JANE RUSSELL

All grandmothers like letters. Even if they just
consist of a squiggle and a dirty finger mark.

PAM BROWN

As someone said, grandchildren "give us pause on the way to heaven." With their arrival, they bring a rush of emotions that sweep over us, temporarily detouring us off the aging track. As soon as we get over the shock of being called "Grandma" many of us find ourselves consumed with new youthful energies and interests we never would have dreamed we'd have: watching cloud formations change or throwing pebbles into ponds or watching squirrels frolic in the treetops.

BARBARA JOHNSON

Our grandchildren accept us for ourselves, without rebuke or effort to change us, as no one in our entire lives has ever done, not our parents, siblings, spouses, friends - and hardly ever our own grown children.

RUTH GOODE

Grandmother and grandchild discussing a common interest are exactly the same age.

DUANE BIRCH

It's so important to give your children and grandchildren inspiration . . . Teach them to notice, to pay attention, to appreciate, and to be inquisitive. Don't just look, try to see.

IRINA BARONOVA-TENNANT

All children are my children. I teach them the songs and whatever else I can. That's what Grandmothers are for—to teach songs and tell stories and show them the right berries to pick and roots to dig. And also to give them all the love they can stand. No better job in the world than being Grandmother.

LEILA FISHER

In the years I was growing up, there were good times and bad times, but when I presented her [my mother] with three children, our relationship stabilized. There is no doubt that the grandchildren offered her the answer to her prayers: revenge.

ERMA BOMBECK

Wow! Are grandchildren great!
Spoil them rotten—give them back—and
laugh and laugh. Revenge is sweet.

ARIS PAINTER

One of life's greatest mysteries is how the boy who
wasn't good enough to marry your daughter can be
the father of the smartest grandchild in the world.

JEWISH PROVERB

You don't think it's possible to love
your grandchildren any more than you do
today . . . but then tomorrow comes.

ANONYMOUS

May you live to enjoy your grandchildren.

PSALM 128:6A

A child needs a grandma to spoil him a bit,
Someone with time on her hands who will sit
In an old-fashioned rocker that shivers and squeaks
And listens to words that a little boy speaks.

ANONYMOUS

If you see a book, a rocking chair, and a grandchild
in the same room, don't pass up the chance to read
aloud. Instill in your grandchild a love of reading.
It's one of the greatest gifts that you can give.

BARBARA BUSH

To become a grandmother is to be suddenly
piercingly aware of the brevity of human life.

CHARLOTTE GRAY

A mother becomes a true grandmother the day she
stops noticing the terrible things her children do
because she is so enchanted with the wonderful
things her grandchildren do.

LOIS WYSE

You know, I think I really was meant to be
a grandmother. It was mothering that
confused me all those years.

PAT, GRANDMOTHER

I have enjoyed greatly the second blooming that
comes when you finish the life of the emotions
and of personal relations; and suddenly find—at
the age of fifty, say—that a whole new life has
opened before you, filled with things you can
think about, study, or read about...It is as if a fresh
sap of ideas and thoughts was rising in you.

AGATHA CHRISTIE

Perhaps one has to be very old before one learns
to be amused rather than shocked.

PEARL S. BUCK

The age of a woman doesn't mean a thing. The best tunes are played on the oldest fiddles.

SIGMUND Z. ENGEL

The feeling of grandparents for their grandchildren can be expressed this way: "Our children are dear to us; but when we have grandchildren, they seem to be more dear than our children were." You might say that the grandmother falls all over herself to try to show her appreciation for her grandchild. It goes right back to those wishes that were made for them when they were little girls: the wish that they would live to become grandmothers someday.

HENRY OLD COYOTE

Grandmothers are voices of the past
and role models of the present. Grandmothers
open the doors to the future.

HELEN KETCHUM

Old-fashioned grandmothers take their grandchildren
by the hand and lead them into the future. They are
safe and kind, and wiser than the child's mother.

FLORENCE KING

They [grandchildren] link us to our own
motherhood and childhood years, to our
parents and grandparents and the stories
we remember of times even earlier than
those. And they link us to the future as
well. They give us a vested interest in
the world in which they will live. They
make us aware of the world in which we
are living today and helping to create for
tomorrow.

RUTH GOODE

## A GRANDMOTHER'S
## PRIDE AND PREJUDICE

God, she's more excited about the birth of her
grandchild than she was about the arrival of
any of her own children. This time around, all
gain, no pain. All pride, sheer prejudice.
Please protect her family.
The little ones, who link her to the future.
The bigger ones, who push them in prams
and cuddle them in bosoms and pray for them
through the night.

EVELYN BENCE

I am rich with years, a millionaire! I have been part of my own generation, then I watched my children's generation grow up, then my grandchildren's and now my great-grandchildren's.

DELORES GARCIA

Grandmas outlast tyrants.
That's why the world survives.

ANONYMOUS

Treat the earth well; it was not given to you by your parents, it was loaned to you by your children. We do not inherit the Earth from our ancestors, we borrow it from our children.

NATIVE AMERICAN PROVERB

Children are the only form of immortality
that we can be sure of.

PETER USTINOV

Our children are not going to be just "our children"—
they are going to be other people's husbands and
wives and the parents of our grandchildren.

MARY S. CALDERONE

Grandmas hold our tiny hands for just a
little while . . . but our hearts forever.

ANONYMOUS